Seeing
Him
More
Clearly

JESUS

Interactions Small Group Series

InterActions
small group series

Seeing
Him
More
Clearly

JESUS

BILL HYBELS
WITH KEVIN AND SHERRY HARNEY

ZONDERVAN™

GRAND RAPIDS, MICHIGAN 49530 USA

WILLOW
Willow Creek Resources

ZONDERVAN™

Jesus
Copyright © 1997 by Willow Creek Association

Requests for information should be addressed to:

Zondervan, *Grand Rapids, Michigan 49530*

ISBN-10: 0-310-26597-5
ISBN-13: 978-0-310-26597-9

Interior design by Rick Devon and Michelle Espinoza

Printed in the United States of America

05 06 07 08 09 10 11 12 /❖ DCI/ 10 9 8 7 6 5 4 3 2 1

CONTENTS

INTERACTIONS

In 1992, Willow Creek Community Church, in partnership with Zondervan and the Willow Creek Association, released a curriculum for small groups entitled the Walking with God series. In just three years, almost a half million copies of these small group study guides were being used in churches around the world. The phenomenal response to this curriculum affirmed the need for relevant and biblical small group materials.

At the writing of this curriculum, there are nearly 3,000 small groups meeting regularly within the structure of Willow Creek Community Church. We believe this number will increase as we continue to place a central value on small groups. Many other churches throughout the world are growing in their commitment to small group ministries as well, so the need for resources is increasing.

In response to this great need, the Interactions small group series has been developed. Willow Creek Association and Zondervan have joined together to create a whole new approach to small group materials. These discussion guides are meant to challenge group members to a deeper level of sharing, to create lines of accountability, to move followers of Christ into action, and to help group members become fully devoted followers of Christ.

SUGGESTIONS FOR INDIVIDUAL STUDY

1. Begin each session with prayer. Ask God to help you understand the passage and to apply it to your life.
2. A good modern translation, such as the New International Version, the New American Standard Bible, or the New Revised Standard Version, will give you the most help. Questions in this guide are based on the New International Version.
3. Read and reread the passage(s). You must know what the passage says before you can understand what it means and how it applies to you.
4. Write your answers in the spaces provided in the study guide. This will help you to express clearly your understanding of the passage.
5. Keep a Bible dictionary handy. Use it to look up unfamiliar words, names, or places.

SUGGESTIONS FOR GROUP STUDY

1. Come to the session prepared. Careful preparation will greatly enrich your time in group discussion.
2. Be willing to join in the discussion. The leader of the group will not be lecturing, but will encourage people to discuss what they have learned in the passage. Plan to share what God has taught you in your individual study.
3. Stick to the passage being studied. Base your answers on the verses being discussed rather than on outside authorities such as commentaries or your favorite author or speaker.
4. Try to be sensitive to the other members of the group. Listen attentively when they speak, and be affirming whenever you can. This will encourage more hesitant members of the group to participate.
5. Be careful not to dominate the discussion. By all means participate, but allow others to have equal time.
6. If you are the discussion leader, you will find additional suggestions and helpful ideas in the Leader's Notes.

ADDITIONAL RESOURCES AND TEACHING MATERIALS

At the end of this study guide you will find a collection of resources and teaching materials to help you in your growth as a follower of Christ. You will also find resources that will help your church develop and build fully devoted followers of Christ.

Introduction: Seeing Him More Clearly

It seems political campaigning never ends these days. Candidates are continually trying to devise strategies that will net them the needed votes to make it through the primaries and into the race for their respective offices.

Some candidates rely almost entirely on the media for their strategy; others bargain and horse-trade in smoke-filled rooms. But sooner or later, every candidate must walk into the crowds, smile broadly, shake hands, and kiss babies. It's what's expected.

One campaign strategy that has always fascinated me is what is called the "identification strategy." You've seen it before and you'll see it again and again. It's when a candidate on the campaign trail visits a place like an automotive assembly plant in Detroit. Are pictures coming to your mind already? What does the candidate do? He or she puts on safety glasses, a hard hat, a company smock, and some work boots, and then stands next to a group of workers for ten to fifteen minutes, posing for the media, making casual conversation and attempting to bolt something together in a rather clumsy fashion. But as soon as the television lights dim, they hustle out for the next scheduled stop.

What's so fascinating about this identification strategy? Well, frankly, I'm rather amazed at the reaction of the workers in the plant. It would seem to me that those workers would resent this obvious political ploy. You would think that more of the workers would say, "Don't pretend that ten or fifteen minutes with us is going to give you any real understanding of what it's like to work on an assembly line. Don't think you can lead us to believe you came here because you really care for us. You want votes, and this is one way to get them." We might expect these workers to tell the candidates, "You're not identifying with us. You're using us."

But it goes on election year after election year, and apparently it's effective. Whether a candidate stands on an assembly line in Detroit or climbs on a tractor in Des Moines or visits a computer plant in Silicon Valley, this political strategy seems to be widely accepted.

I actually get the impression that most workers in those places are satisfied with the illusion that the candidate was trying to understand their work situation and express care and concern. It's almost as if they're saying to the candidate, "You may or may not be for real, you may or may not actually care about our situation, but at least you showed up. You came here in person. You stood on our level. You wore our company logo, our smock and safety glasses, just like us. You put on the illusion of identification for a few minutes, and that's better than being ignored."

I've wondered from time to time if any of those candidates would actually be willing to take a job on one of those assembly lines for six months or a year. Would any of those candidates actually be willing to work next to these people? to receive their paychecks? to eat in their lunchrooms? to ride in their cars? to live in their homes? I think most candidates would gladly settle for the illusion of identification.

God decided He would not settle for the illusion of identification when He sent His Son to this planet. He didn't request that Jesus come down, make a low pass, and return to heaven untouched and uninvolved. Jesus didn't come to pose for the press and the media for ten or fifteen minutes and leave when the lights and cameras went off. Jesus didn't ponder the incredible humiliation and suffering He would have to endure and then decide to play it safe and settle for an illusion of identification. God's divine plan in bringing Jesus to earth was to demonstrate to the whole world, for all of time, the purest outpouring of care and concern anyone would ever be able to imagine.

It is difficult for us to completely come to grips with the words of Philippians 2:6–7. Here's a paraphrase: "Although Jesus existed in the form of God, He did not regard His standing with God, His equality with God, as something to be grasped or clutched onto. Rather, He was willing to set aside His heavenly prerogatives to take on the form of a bond servant. He was willing to become a man."

While it is true that Jesus Christ came to save us from our sin and to bring us salvation, there's another, often overlooked, purpose for God putting on human flesh in the form of Jesus Christ. It was for identification—not the illusion of identification, but to provide us with the epitome of identification. It would be like a candidate relinquishing all of his money, degrees, fame, and fortune, and committing himself to work the rest of his life on the assembly line. Jesus walked this earth as one of us.

In essence, God was saying, "I'm not only going to give you a Savior, someone for your soul, someone to prepare you for the afterlife, but I'm providing you with a sympathetic Savior, a Savior who understands, One who you can identify with, feel close to, talk with, learn to love. One who is going to make a difference in your life every day."

These six sessions will help you see this Savior more clearly. When He walked on this earth, Jesus revealed Himself as a man, a great teacher, a physician, a servant, a good shepherd, and a king. When combined, these portraits give us a full picture of who Jesus Christ is, and why He left heaven to live and die on earth. He did not settle for the illusion of identification . . . He came as one of us.

Bill Hybels

JESUS THE MAN

I think one of the most painful and uncomfortable feelings a human being can experience is the feeling of loneliness. If we could carefully peel back what is really going on when a person says, "I feel lonely or isolated," we would often find at the core of those claims one recurring phrase: "No one understands how I feel." We have all felt it, and most of us have said it on various occasions. In life's painful moments, we all have a sense that no one understands where we are coming from, how we hurt inside, or what we are feeling.

One of the loneliest times of my life was shortly after the unexpected death of my father, who died suddenly of a heart attack. My wife was very kind through those painful and heart-numbing days, as were many others. Several people from Willow Creek drove 175 miles to stand with me alongside my dad's grave. It was a very moving experience.

However, even in the midst of all this care, I remember feeling over and over that nobody really understood what I was going through. It didn't help much when some well-meaning person would come and say, "Bill, I know what you are feeling. My Aunt Edna died several years ago and I still miss her. I know what it's like." I would think, "I know you mean well, but you just don't understand." Through that time of grieving I learned a principle I have tried not to violate since. When people lose loved ones, I never say to them, "I understand." Now I go to people and say, "I'm sure I can't understand how much you must have loved your dad or wife or child. I'm sure I don't understand all you are feeling. But I do love you, and I'm here for you."

We can pray, cry, and listen to those in need, but deep down in every person is the yearning to have someone, somewhere, understand us perfectly and totally. We all hunger to have one person who knows just how we feel and who will never leave us in the middle of the hard times. The good news is that Jesus Christ is that person. As the old hymn says, "No one understands like Jesus."

A WIDE ANGLE VIEW

1 Describe a time you felt like no one could understand what you were going through. How did realizing that Christ understood your pain help you through this time?

A BIBLICAL PORTRAIT

Read Philippians 2:5–11

2 When Jesus left the glory of heaven to be born in a stable and live as a human being, what did He give up?

3 From this passage and your knowledge of the life of Jesus, what pain and suffering did Christ experience when He walked on this earth as a man:

- Emotionally

- Physically

- Relationally

- Spiritually

SHARPENING THE FOCUS

Read Snapshot "Jesus Understands Relationships"

JESUS UNDERSTANDS RELATIONSHIPS

I would guess that few of us have spent much time pondering the fact that Jesus was born into a family. He knew what it was like to have parents, brothers, and sisters. He knew what it was like to be a baby, a toddler, a young child, an adolescent, and an adult who interacted with others. Jesus also knew what it was like to have friends. Peter, James, and John are often identified as close friends of Jesus, and He also had intimate friendships with Lazarus, Mary, Martha, and many others.

You might say, "Why does this matter? How does this impact me?" Well, from time to time, most of us cry out in frustration, "No one understands what it's like to face what I am facing." Young people say, "My parents have long forgotten, my teachers don't care, and my friends are having the same problems I'm having. Nobody understands. There's no help." As adults, we can feel like no one understands when our relationships are in turmoil. When this happens you can say, "No one understands," but you need to add two more words: "like Jesus." Jesus has been there. He's walked that path. No one understands like Jesus.

4 In 1 Peter 5:7 we hear this invitation, "Cast all your anxiety on him because he cares for you." Tell about a time you cast your anxieties and problems on Jesus concerning a relationship. How did you sense His care for you?

5 What is one relationship in your life that is broken or is not what you feel it should be?

What can your group members do to support you as you seek healing in this relationship?

Read Snapshot "Jesus Understands Work"

JESUS UNDERSTANDS WORK

Did you ever stop to think that Jesus was a carpenter for a greater period of time than He was a teacher and preacher? He spent more time in the marketplace than He did in the temple. I think He was probably more at home in a woodshop than He was in a religious workshop or seminar. And I'm sure He had more contacts socially because of His carpentry trade than He had because of His religious involvements. In Mark 6:3 we read that people referred to Jesus as "the carpenter." He was not just the son of a carpenter, but was recognized as an accomplished carpenter in His own right.

In that day for someone to be a carpenter meant being highly skilled, multitalented, and callous-handed. The fact that Jesus was a carpenter meant He knew all about exhaustion after a full day's work. He knew all about frustration because of rain, snow, broken tools, and pay disputes. And He certainly knew the battle with monotony and boredom when He had to make thousands of bricks day after day.

Because of this, Jesus knows all about what it means to live with the many frustrations that come with our daily work. He knows about our marketplace temptations, frustrations, and pressures. He's been there. He understands.

---

6 In what ways are you feeling bogged down, frustrated, or at the end of your rope with your work?

Take some time as a group to pray for these concerns
expressed. Remember, "No one understands like Jesus."

Read Snapshot "Jesus Understands Pain and Suffering"

JESUS UNDERSTANDS PAIN AND SUFFERING

God had no intentions of shielding His Son from pain and suffering. All the way back in the book of Isaiah, centuries before the birth of Jesus, the prophet predicted that the Messiah would be "despised and rejected by men, a man of sorrows, and familiar with suffering" (Isa. 53:3). Right from the first day of Jesus' public ministry the ridicule began. People said, "He's a carpenter, a blue-collar worker! The Messiah can't come from a blue-collar family!" People also remarked, "What good comes from Nazareth?" and critics mocked and questioned Jesus' claim of virgin birth. And, finally, Jesus was a Jew during the time of Roman occupation, so people ridiculed Him because of His race.

Jesus also knew about rejection. His own brothers didn't even believe in Him until after His resurrection. One of the twelve disciples, Judas, betrayed Jesus with a kiss, and His other disciples deserted Him in His hour of greatest need. The people Jesus was dying to save were the very same people who shouted, "Crucify Him! Kill Him!" And then, in that hour on the cross, when Jesus bore our sins on Himself, God the Father Himself rejected His very own Son, leaving Jesus to cry out, "My God, My God, why have You forsaken Me?"

And finally, Jesus knew all about physical pain. He was beaten, flogged, scourged, slapped, and crowned with thorns. The cross He would die on was strapped to His back and He had to carry it to the place of His public execution. Nails were driven into His hands and feet, and a sword was plunged into His side. The phrase "familiar with suffering" may indeed be the understatement of history.

7

Jesus suffered pain, rejection, and humiliation so that we might be able to receive forgiveness for all our sins. How do you feel when you realize Jesus endured unimaginable suffering and pain because He loves you and wanted to offer you salvation?

8 Describe one area of your life in which you are experiencing pain and suffering at this time.

What can your small group members do to support you in this area?

PUTTING YOURSELF IN THE PICTURE

MEETING JESUS IN HIS SUFFERING

In the coming week, read Matthew 26–28. Take time to reflect on the following questions:

- What did Jesus suffer as He gave His life for me?
- What would I have to experience if I had to pay for my own sins?
- What can I do to express my appreciation for all Jesus did for me when He came to this earth as a man?

EXTENDING JESUS' LOVE TO THE HURTING

Identify one person you know who is going through a difficult time and needs support and encouragement. Commit yourself to do three things:

- Pray for that person to experience God's strength and care in the coming days.

- Through a phone call, a letter, or face-to-face contact, communicate to that person what you have learned in this study about how Jesus understands what they are facing.
- Find one specific action you can do to help lighten that person's load and lift his or her burden.

Be sure one member of your small group is praying for you as you minister to this person. Ask this group member to keep you accountable to follow through on this commitment in the coming weeks.

JESUS THE TEACHER

REFLECTIONS FROM SESSION 1

1. If you took time to study Matthew 26–28 since your last group meeting, tell your group members what you learned about the suffering of Jesus.
2. If you set a goal to extend the love of Jesus to a hurting person, tell your group about this experience and how it impacted both you and the person you reached out to.

THE BIG PICTURE

Matthew 7:28 says, "When Jesus had finished saying these things, the crowds were *amazed* at his teaching." Matthew 13:54 says, "Coming to his hometown, he began teaching the people in their synagogue, and they were *amazed*. 'Where did this man get this wisdom and these miraculous powers?' they asked." After Jesus was cross-examined by the experts in Mosaic law, Matthew 22:33 says, "When the crowds heard this, they were *astonished* at his teaching." And in John 7:46, we read that even the temple guards of the Pharisees confessed, "No one ever spoke the way this man does."

Friend or foe, believer or atheist, it seems everyone agrees about at least one aspect of the life of Jesus of Nazareth: He was among the greatest teachers who ever lived. Most, in fact, would call Him *the* greatest teacher, the Master Teacher.

The term "teacher" was not tossed around lightly in those days, yet Jesus was referred to as "the teacher" more than forty times throughout the Gospels. Thousands of people followed Him into the desert, into the countryside, into the mountains, and along the seashore, hungering to hear Him preach, teach, and speak of the things of God.

Very few preachers or teachers have this problem today. Most teachers have to work overtime to get people to come to their classes, seminars, or church services. Jesus was indeed a master teacher who knew the incredible impact of the spoken word and the powerful influence a teacher has on all those who will listen.

A WIDE ANGLE VIEW

1 Who was one teacher (in church or in school) who made a significant impact on your life?

What was it about that teacher that influenced you?

A BIBLICAL PORTRAIT

The three passages listed below are taken from a message commonly called "The Sermon on the Mount." It is considered by many to be the greatest sermon ever preached. As you listen to these sections being read, allow the message to impact your life, but also seek to gain insight into the One who first spoke these words with clarity and power.

Read Matthew 5:3–12; 6:5–15; 7:24–27

2 In Matthew 5:3–12 we see an upside-down view of life. How do these words of Jesus fly in the face of today's conventional wisdom?

3

According to Jesus' teaching, how are we to pray?

What should we avoid when praying?

SHARPENING THE FOCUS

Read Snapshot "Jesus Taught with Authority"

JESUS TAUGHT WITH AUTHORITY

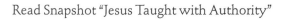

Why did Jesus' teachings attract so many people? One reason is that Jesus spoke authoritatively. Often after Jesus taught we read words like, "The people were amazed at his teaching, because he taught them as one who had authority, not as the teachers of the law" (Mark 1:22). One of the more clever and memorable ads on television some years ago made a simple statement: "When E. F. Hutton talks . . . people listen!" Well, when Jesus Christ spoke, people listened—and trembled. They stood in awe. Their hearts melted as He spoke, because He spoke with authority. There was an unmistakable tone of certitude in His voice, an intrinsic power communicated by His person, a sense of finality about His words. At times Jesus would say, "You have heard that it was said . . . But I say to you . . ." as if everything said up to this point mattered little in comparison to what He was going to say. Now, that's authority.

4

In John 14:6 Jesus said, "I am the way and the truth and the life. No one comes to the Father except through me." What would you say to a person who states, "Jesus never meant to say He was the only way to God. We all know there are many ways to heaven"?

5 Not only did Jesus teach with authority when He walked on the earth, He continues to teach with authority today. How are you seeking to follow the authoritative teaching of Jesus in your life today?

Read Snapshot "Jesus Taught Graphically"

JESUS TAUGHT GRAPHICALLY

Another reason for Jesus' effectiveness is that He spoke graphically. Jesus spoke truth, but not in colorless platitudes. He didn't say, "The following is a list of 245 timeless truths in order of importance." Jesus knew two thousand years ago what language experts and developmental psychologists are just discovering now—people think in pictures more than in sentences. With this in mind, Jesus painted pictures with His words.

Once when Jesus was teaching He said, in effect, "Think of a huge log, a great big log. Got it? Now, imagine this. Stick that log in your eye. And then stick another log in your other eye." At this point the people must have been laughing and saying, "The log is bigger than my head. How do I fit it in my eye?" Those hearing Jesus' message could picture themselves stumbling around, basically blind from planks of wood in their eyes.

Jesus continued, "Imagine that you bump into a friend who has a little speck of sawdust in his eye. Think of how foolish it would be for you, with logs in your eyes, to try to help him get the little speck out of his eye." And people must have been thinking, "You're right. That would be pretty stupid." Then Jesus said, "Here is what you have to do. You have to take the logs out of your own eyes first. And after your eyes are clear, you can help your friend get the speck of sawdust out of his eye." Finally, He said, "I suggest that all you people stop judging one another until you are willing to repent of your own sin first. Until you are ready to bow to God and seek forgiveness and walk in purity and holiness yourself, don't try to take a little speck out of someone else's eye when you have logs in your own."

6 What is it about the language of these stories that allows them to stick with us?

7 What is one "log in your eye" that you need to remove before pointing out other people's "specks"?

Read Snapshot "Jesus Taught Practically"

JESUS TAUGHT PRACTICALLY

 Jesus did not speak in esoteric generalities. His teaching was always practical and called people to action. "Wayward sons, come home and receive forgiveness from your Father," He would command. Or, "Brothers and sisters who are warring with each other, don't go to church and play religious games. Drop whatever you're doing and try to be reconciled with your brother or your sister." Or, "Stop worrying about tomorrow. Worry is a waste of time. Rather, trust in Me." Or, "Feed the poor, clothe the naked, care for the afflicted. Show special concern for little children. Seek first the kingdom of God." Can you see what's happening here? Jesus is telling, without apology, how a follower of Christ should think, act, and live. And then He is saying, "Now, go do it!"

8

When has the teaching of Jesus touched you in a clear and practical way? What action did this teaching move you to and how did this impact your life as a follower of Christ?

9

What is one teaching of Jesus that is a cutting edge in your life at this time?

What has He taught you and what change is He seeking to bring in your life?

How can your group members pray for you, support you, and keep you on track as you grow in this area of your life?

PUTTING YOURSELF IN THE PICTURE

HEARING JESUS SPEAK THROUGH THE BIBLE

One way you can receive a personal message from God is through reading and meditating on the Bible. If you commit yourself to reading just a little portion of the Bible each day, your life will never be the same. Whether you need a word of comfort, encouragement, peace, approval, forgiveness, or assurance, always remember that the primary way God communicates is through the Scriptures. Commit yourself to reading a specific amount of time each day for the coming two weeks and see how God begins speaking to you. Jesus still wants to teach all those who will listen to Him.

Determine a pattern of Bible reading and reflection for the coming two weeks.

What book or section of the Bible will you begin with?
Share your plans with another person in your group. Call each other during the week to see how it is going.

HEARING GOD'S VOICE

God also speaks, from time to time, directly through His Holy Spirit to your heart. This may sound incredibly mystical but the truth of the matter is, Romans 8:15–16 says,

> For you did not receive a spirit that makes you a slave again to fear, but you received the Spirit of sonship. And by him we cry, "*Abba*, Father." The Spirit himself testifies with our spirit that we are God's children.

This passage gives precedence for a phenomenon that mature believers have come to know and appreciate. Sometimes in the middle of a believer's day, while in the car, in the office, at home, walking, eating, reading, or going about their business, God makes an impression on the heart of a believer. By the Holy Spirit, God communicates something to His follower. He may say, "I love you" or "I'm here. I just wanted you to know that I'm right here with you." Or He might say, "Don't worry. I know you're getting uptight right now, but I don't want you to worry. I've got everything under control." Or maybe, "You're doing a great job right now. Well done, good and faithful servant." Take time in the coming week to quiet your heart and invite God to speak gently to you.

INVITING GOD TO SPEAK THROUGH OTHERS

God can also communicate to us through other believers. Some of God's most meaningful words can come through other people. God can speak through casual conversations with family members, church members, friends, or anyone who is available to be used by Him. As you spend time with other Christians, God may choose, through the life of another believer, to speak to you the very word you need to hear. Take time in the coming week to pray for two specific things:

1. Pray for God to speak to you through His Spirit.
2. Pray for a heart that is open to hear what God wants to say through others.

In the coming week, use the space provided below to write down anything you feel God has tried to communicate to you through others, or a prompting you have sensed from His Spirit.

JESUS THE PHYSICIAN

REFLECTIONS FROM SESSION 2

1. If you developed a plan for reading and reflection, how did that plan work out? Describe to your group members what insights God has been teaching you. How has the discipline of reading the Bible made a difference in your life?
2. If you have been quieting your heart and seeking to hear the Holy Spirit lead you, tell the group what God has been saying to you.
3. If you have been asking God to speak to you through others over the past week(s), tell your small group members how God has taught you through the life and words of another believer.

THE BIG PICTURE

David Gilmore and his wife, Tammy, never considered calling a doctor when their fifteen-month-old son, Graham, became seriously ill in April of '78. "At first it was like the flu, and we didn't think anything of it," Gilmore said. "We did what we were taught to do. We prayed." But the flu-like symptoms lingered for a week, and Graham's temperature climbed. Though the Gilmores didn't know it at the time, their son had meningitis, a dangerous inflammation of the membranes that enveloped the brain and spinal cord.

"My mother heard Graham was sick and came down to see him," Gilmore said. "She must have realized something was seriously wrong, because a couple days later my sister called and said to me, 'Davey, I know you're trying to do the right thing, but it won't hurt your faith if you let me take the baby to the doctor, will it?'"

Gilmore politely refused, and then got angry when his sister asked him if Graham could hear. "I told her of course he can hear me. What kind of a question is that? I hung up on her, walked over to the couch where Graham was lying, and snapped my fingers. He just looked straight ahead. He never moved. I clapped my hands and started yelling and jumping up and down, and he kept looking off into space. He couldn't hear me. He was deaf."

Even then, Gilmore said, neither he nor his wife became worried. They called a friend who reassured them that the deafness was only a lie of the devil, and that their faith was being tested. The friend urged them to take the baby and their older daughter away for a few days. "We checked into a Holiday Inn in Goshen, Indiana, and were all set to go swimming when Tammy, my wife, called to me and said, 'He can't see now. He can't even see.' She was right. Graham had become blind. He couldn't see anything." Gilmore packed up the family and drove back to their home. Although they were upset, Gilmore and his wife still had faith.

They refused to call a doctor and continued to pray over their blind and deaf infant son for another week, while his condition worsened and his jaw muscles locked and his neck swelled. Gilmore tells what happened next.

"Then on Sunday we went to church in the morning, and again at night. We took Graham. That's the weird thing. We believed that if a child is sick and you pray for him, he is already healed. He really isn't sick, even though he appears to be." Gilmore said the pastor gave a particularly rousing sermon about faith that night, and he and his wife returned home feeling better. Their feelings rose even higher when Graham, who was still nursing, ate some cereal. "We were soaring," Gilmore said. "When we went to bed we were so happy. Then in the morning, when we got up, Graham was blue. He was stiff. He was dead." It was May 15, 1978.

The Gilmores were also told that the same power of prayer that heals the sick also raises the dead. So David and Tammy Gilmore decided to take their faith one step farther and pray for the resurrection of their son. "We got down on our knees at the foot of the bed," David Gilmore said. "After fifteen minutes of prayer I just knew I couldn't go on one more minute. I look back on it now and realize I was just gone. I was lost." Gilmore said his son's death tore the heart out of his wife. The worst pain came, he said, when they asked the doctor if Graham's condition might have been treatable. "The doctor told us that it was the type of meningitis that could have been easily cured if we had gone to him early enough."

A WIDE ANGLE VIEW

1 What is your gut reaction to this story and why do you think you react this way?

How do you respond to this statement: "We should appreciate the fact that this couple was trying to live out their faith and convictions!"

A BIBLICAL PORTRAIT

Read Luke 5:12–16

2 What insight do you gain into the heart of Jesus through this passage?

3 What do you notice about Jesus' approach to healing and His healing style from this passage and other passages which tell of the healing ministry of Jesus?

Read Snapshot "Beware of Sensationalists"

BEWARE OF SENSATIONALISTS

Most so-called "healing ministries" today can be put into the following categories. The first category of healing ministries I call the sensationalists. These healers have a style almost completely opposite that of Jesus. He was compassionate, personal, and liked to do things in private. He healed for the sake of the afflicted one, and gave all credit heavenward.

In stark contrast, most sensationalist healers tend to be strangely impersonal. Often they don't bother with names and background information. In fact, many of these healers are involved in mail-order healings. A person can send in for some trinket that has been touched by the healer, and this item is supposed to be a catalyst for the person's healing. Sensationalist healers can also be embarrassingly conscious of lighting and camera angles and unusually rude to the public. Many of them seem to be deeply committed to impressing a constituency and curiously willing to call attention to themselves and their "ministry."

---

4 The sensationalist approach to healing can be hurtful to those who are sick, turn off seekers, and damage the health of the church. How have you seen people hurt through this approach to healing?

Read Snapshot "Beware of Confessionalists"

BEWARE OF CONFESSIONALISTS

There's another type of healing ministry going on today that I call "confessionalism." This approach to healing teaches that it is always God's will that all afflicted people be healed, and that all God is waiting for is for the afflicted person to demonstrate enough faith. Those who are afflicted are encouraged to confess their faith verbally by saying, "I have been healed. I am in great health. I have a restored body because of the power of Jesus Christ." Leaders of this type of healing ministry feel that if people confess their faith in this way enough times, they will believe they are healed, and by believing, they will receive the healing.

5

"I guess you don't have enough faith" is the response of confessionalists to those who fail to become healed. What does this view of healing do to the faith of Christ's followers who pray for healing but don't experience it?

Read Snapshot "God Can't Do That"

GOD CAN'T DO THAT

A third group of people, sometimes called "cessationalists" (meaning all healing has ceased) say, "Healings and miracles aren't for this age or this dispensation." They admit that Jesus healed when He walked on this earth. They even acknowledge that the first-century disciples and other leaders did miraculous healings. But they insist that there are no more healings or miracles today. An eerie type of fatalism often accompanies this type of thinking. Leaders say, "God loves us, but healing is not for this time of history."

6

How does this view of divine healing impact those who are sick and suffering?

Read Snapshot "A Balanced View of Healing"

A BALANCED VIEW OF HEALING

The truth is, God continues to heal today. God has created our bodies with a wonderful ability to fight off sickness and to heal after injuries. When His power brings us healing through natural means, we should give Him thanks. We should also be deeply grateful for the help God brings through the skill of doctors.

Along with natural and medical healing, sometimes God decides to remove an illness, strengthen a heart, and bring healing by miraculous means. In James chapter five, we learn that the afflicted person should call for the elders of the church. Everyone involved in the healing—the person pursuing the healing as well as the elders—should thoroughly confess their sins. Then there should be anointing of oil, which is a symbol of the operation and presence of the Holy Spirit, followed by faithful prayer.

7

How have you seen God heal through *one* of the following means:

- Natural means
- Medical means
- His miraculous and supernatural power

8

Who is one person in your life who needs to experience the healing power of God today?

Handwritten notes:

Carol -
allergic -
to pain
meds

Doug's mom
Mark's mom
Franchesca - in labor
since Mon.

Brandi's friend - 4 kids
husb. left
Neidig's - 1yr anniv. of grand
Ted Snyder kid's
Paul Zimmerman death

Take time as a group to pray for these people.

PUTTING YOURSELF IN THE PICTURE

A CLOSER LOOK AT THE GREAT PHYSICIAN

Take time in the coming weeks to read the entire gospel of Luke. Keep a list of all the times Jesus went one-on-one with a person who needed healing. Note as many details as possible regarding where, when, how, and why the encounter happened. What went on just before the healing and what came after it? Committing to this study will likely be one of the richest Bible studies you've ever done.

THE PRAYER OF FAITH

Take time in the coming days to memorize James 5:13–16:

> Is any one of you in trouble? He should pray. Is anyone happy? Let him sing songs of praise. Is any one of you sick? He should call the elders of the church to pray over him and anoint him with oil in the name of the Lord. And the prayer offered in faith will make the sick person well; the Lord will raise him up. If he has sinned, he will be forgiven. Therefore

confess your sins to each other and pray for each other so that you may be healed. The prayer of a righteous man is powerful and effective.

A Closing Note . . . Sometimes God Says No

Sometimes God heals through natural means, sometimes through medical means, sometimes through prayer and a direct touch. But we must never forget that sometimes God says no to a healing. He said no to Paul, and He has said no to thousands of others throughout history. You might ask, "Why would an all-loving, all-powerful God say no to the healing of afflicted persons?" I think the best answer is found in Isaiah 55:8. In this passage God says, "For my thoughts are not your thoughts, neither are your ways my ways. . . . As the heavens are higher than the earth, so are my ways higher than your ways, and my thoughts than your thoughts."

JESUS THE SERVANT

REFLECTIONS FROM SESSION 3

1. If you have been studying the gospel of Luke and taking a closer look at the healing ministry of Jesus, tell your group members what you have been learning and how this impacts your understanding of Jesus and your relationship with Him.
2. If you memorized James 5:13–16, how has this experience impacted your faith and your prayers?

THE BIG PICTURE

Wilbur Reese writes:

I would like to buy three dollars worth of God, please.
Not enough to explode my soul or disturb my sleep,
But just enough to equal a cup of warm milk, or a snooze in the sunshine.
I don't want enough of Him to make me love a black man,
or pick beets with a migrant worker.
I want ecstasy, not transformation.
I want the warmth of the womb, not a new birth.
I want a pound of the eternal in a paper sack.
I would like to buy three dollars worth of God, please.

Reese writes these words tongue in cheek, but his point comes through loud and clear. There are times in all of our lives when we want just "three dollars worth of God." Who doesn't prefer ecstasy and euphoria to commitment and self-sacrifice? Who doesn't want peace like a river rather than the rapids and white water of following Christ no matter what the cost. Most of us would tend toward the security and the warmth of the womb rather than a cataclysmic rebirth.

A WIDE ANGLE VIEW

1

How do you respond to Reese's poem?

In what ways do people want "three dollars worth of God" today?

A BIBLICAL PORTRAIT

Read John 13:1–17

2

What do you learn about serving others from this passage?

3

What do you learn about the heart of Jesus in this passage?

What do you learn about the heart of His disciples?

SHARPENING THE FOCUS

Read Snapshot "Me-ism"

ME-ISM

We live in a me-centered world. Me-ism has a devastating effect on marriage and family life. Someone who is me-istic views his or her spouse as someone to meet their needs rather than a person to love and nurture. And parents who get me-istic consider their children an interruption rather than an investment.

Me-ism is also rampant in the workplace. It causes the traditional management versus labor battles. Management says, "We own the company. We run it. And we want the profits." Labor says, "We work hard, so we want higher pay, fewer hours, and more benefits." The war goes on as the warriors lift up the battle cry, "Me! Me! Me!"

Me-ism is even rampant in the church. Many people attend a church because it makes them feel good. Their primary concern is what they gain from the experience.

This me-ism in our culture is often accentuated by the media. "You deserve a break today." "You need this car." "Have it your way." "Do yourself a favor." Today, it is very easy to get sucked into the pattern of seeking first the things *we* want.

4 What are some of the signs of me-ism you see in *one* of these areas:

- In the media
- In the church
- In business
- In your community
- In your own life

5 Where do you see the battle of me-ism raging in you?

Pause as a group to pair off. Confess your me-isms to one another and pray for each other.

Read Snapshot "Jesus the Servant"

JESUS THE SERVANT

 Jesus taught servanthood. In His day the Jews were anticipating a strong, militaristic, royal Messiah to come and deliver them from Roman oppression. They were delirious with excitement at the thought of a God-sent monarch who would free them from Roman rule. But the Old Testament prophets declared that the Messiah would come in the form of a servant. He would come to liberate from sin, not from Rome. He would come to serve, heal the sick, feed the hungry, give to the poor. The religious leaders and people of Jesus' day had a hard time grasping the concept of Jesus the Servant.

Even Jesus' disciples stumbled over this basic truth. In Mark 8:31 we read, "He then began to teach them that the Son of Man must suffer many things and be rejected by the elders, chief priests and teachers of the law, and that he must be killed and after three days rise again." And later in Mark 10:45, Jesus said, "For even the Son of Man did not come to be served, but to serve, and to give his life as a ransom for many." Jesus was committed to serve, even if it cost Him His life. And it did.

6

What are some examples of how Jesus lived the life of a servant when He walked on this earth?

7

In John 13 we see Jesus taking the role of a servant and washing His followers' feet. If you had been sitting at the table, Jesus would have gotten on His knees and washed your feet. How do you think you would have responded?

How does it make you feel to know Jesus has served you in ways even greater than washing dirt off your feet?

Read Snapshot "A Call to Service"

A CALL TO SERVICE

Jesus calls us to serve the people in our lives—in our families, in the marketplace, at school, in our neighborhoods, in the church, and wherever we go. Figuratively speaking, we are called to wash each other's feet. Jesus said that servanthood must start with the total overhaul of our hearts and our attitudes. We can't have just three dollars worth of God; we need a total transformation. We need a whole new attitude toward relationships that will lead to new actions. Conventional attitudes of apathy, insensitivity, neglect, and exploitation must be purged from our hearts. Jesus says, "No more business as usual. You have new minds and new attitudes. Now, wash each other's feet." We can't just talk the talk of a servant, we must walk the walk. True servanthood moves us to action.

---

8 What one specific act of service have you felt God prompting you to do, but you have been resisting?

What is keeping you from doing it? What do you need to do to act on this prompting?

9 Who is one person in your life you sense God wants you to begin serving regularly and consistently?

What specific acts of service do you feel called to do for this person?

An Attitude of Service

Take time in the coming week to memorize these two passages:

> For even the Son of Man did not come to be served, but to serve, and to give his life as a ransom for many.
>
> *Mark 10:45*

> Now that I, your Lord and Teacher, have washed your feet, you also should wash one another's feet. I have set you an example that you should do as I have done for you.
>
> *John 13:14–15*

Following Jesus' Example

Commit yourself to putting your faith into action by serving others. Think about the specific act of service and the person who came to your mind when you discussed questions eight and nine in this session. Whom will you serve? When will you serve them? What will you do? As a means of holding each other up, be sure to ask a group member to pray for you to fulfill this commitment to be a servant.

JESUS THE SHEPHERD

REFLECTIONS FROM SESSION 4

1. If you have been memorizing and reflecting on the meaning of Mark 10:45 and John 13:14–15, what have you
   learned about Jesus as a servant and how has this influenced your view of yourself and your commitment to
   live as a servant?
2. If you committed to put your faith into action by setting
   a goal to serve someone, describe how you have done in
   keeping this commitment and what it has taught you
   about being a servant.

THE BIG PICTURE

It matters little who dies. Laborer, manager, spinster, mobster,
pastor, parishioner. In the final moments of unfathomable
grief, almost without exception, one famous chapter of the
Bible is read. That chapter is the Twenty-third Psalm. In my
Bible there's a date written off to the side of Psalm 23. It is
October 7, 1974. There's also the name of a young woman
next to this date: June Stadnicky. I remember her well. She
was twenty-two years old when I met her. She happened to
drop into the church at which I was working while I was
teaching at Son City Ministry back in Park Ridge, Illinois. She
came just two times and committed her life to Jesus Christ.
She was sitting in the back of the church because the services
were primarily for high school students and she did not want
to stand out. She called me and said she had just gone in for a
physical because she was going to get a new job. During the
physical they discovered that she had leukemia. She was
rushed to the hospital, where doctors said she had only three
weeks to live. Sadly, in this case they were right.

I visited June a few times in the coming days, and three
weeks later to the day, she died. She was married and had

two children. I had never done a funeral before, but I was asked to do hers. Her husband was confused. Her children were small and didn't really know what was going on except that something was dreadfully wrong. I remember searching my heart and saying, "What in the world am I going to say at this funeral?" I felt there was nothing I could say that would really make a difference.

That's when I read and studied the Twenty-third Psalm. I discovered there was a lot God could say that would make a dramatic difference. I suppose that was the first time I really fell in love with this psalm. I've read it hundreds of times since, and every time I am reminded of what a great Shepherd we have.

A WIDE ANGLE VIEW

1   If you have ever lost a loved one, describe how you experienced the love and care of God in the middle of that painful time.

A BIBLICAL PORTRAIT

Read Psalm 23

2   What do you discover about the Lord as your Shepherd from this psalm?

He provides what I need: Restores, guides + comforts me; I don't need to fear

How does this make you feel?

3

If we know the Good Shepherd—really know Him—
we will experience all of the things presented in Psalm
23. However, if the Good Shepherd feels more like a
casual acquaintance, we will never experience the relationship vividly described in this psalm. For example,
take each statement in this psalm and insert the word
not. If the Lord is *not* someone's Shepherd, what impact
will this have on them?

no hope; damnation

*How does this affect the way you look at family members and
friends who do not know Jesus Christ, the Good Shepherd?*

SHARPENING THE FOCUS

Read Snapshot "How the Shepherd Provides"

HOW THE SHEPHERD PROVIDES

Every true believer sooner or later comes to grips with the fact that if they have Christ as their personal Savior, they have it all. When Jesus is your Shepherd, every major issue in your life has been set-
tled. You know who you are, where you've come from, where you're going when you die, and what to
do with your life in the meantime. You have guidelines to follow, you know who to befriend, who to
trust, and how to pray. You have forgiveness of sins and assurance of salvation. You have the Holy
Spirit, the resident Truth-Teacher and Guide, living inside you, reminding you of who you are in Christ and giving you
a clear sense of the presence of Jesus Christ. You have the church, God's people, with whom you gather for worship
and build relationships as you learn about support, care, and love. And on top of all of that, you have the promise of
eternal life. When you have Jesus Christ, you have everything you will ever need.

4 When Jesus is your Shepherd, He promises to provide all you need. How have you experienced God's provision in *one* of these areas:

- A sense of contentment, even when you did not have everything you wanted
- Restoration for your heart, even when it was grieving and broken
- Guidance when life's direction seemed hard to find

5 If you had to put your finger on what you need most in your life right now, which of the needs below would it be?

- Contentment
- Restoration for your heart and soul
- Guidance

Why do you need this at this time in your life, and how can your small group support you as you seek to discover this in the Good Shepherd?

Read Snapshot "How the Shepherd Protects"

HOW THE SHEPHERD PROTECTS

Psalm 23 says, "Even though I walk through the valley of the shadow of death, I will fear no evil, for you are with me; your rod and your staff, they comfort me." These verses strike at the heart of one of our most dreaded foes . . . fear! We have all felt it. You might even be feeling it right now. Some people face debilitating, paralyzing, destructive fear that leads to despair and utter immobilization. Every human being is susceptible to it. It comes in various shapes and forms, but it can haunt all of us.

"What if something ever happened to my child?" "What if something happened to my spouse?" "What would I do if I lost my father or mother?" "What if I lost my house, my job, my health . . ." We all live with "what if" questions that bring fear to our hearts and lives.

The Good Shepherd says, "I won't promise to insulate you from all tragedy or loss, but I will protect you from the destructive consequences of it. I'll see you through." There may be bleak nights, but joy will come in the morning. As we walk through the valley of the shadow of death, the Good Shepherd says, "You need not fear. You need not get paranoid. You don't have to fall apart or come undone. I am with you." We must never forget those assuring words, "I am with you."

---

6 King David knew the horrors of battle and war. He knew persecution and family strife beyond what most of us could imagine. Yet in the midst of this, he spoke confidently of God's protection. Tell of a time when you clearly experienced the protection of God in your life.

7 How do you need God's protecting hand to watch over you during this coming week?

Read Snapshot "What the Shepherd Predicts"

WHAT THE SHEPHERD PREDICTS

People are fascinated with predictions. In a futile, misguided effort to know what lies ahead, people read palms, leaves, stars, horoscopes, and even fortune cookies. Unfortunately, tarot cards, dial-a-psychic hotlines, and crystal balls will only disappoint and mislead. However, there is another way to get a clear look into the future. The Good Shepherd has made some arresting predictions—predictions that are going to come true. No $3.99 per minute charges to give us a view to the future; no "operators are standing by." Just straight truth—for free!

Psalm 23 says, "Surely goodness and love will follow me all the days of my life, and I will dwell in the house of the LORD forever." This verse gives two predictions about those who are followers of Christ. First of all, "Surely goodness and love will follow me" is a prediction about the inner quality of your life. The word "follow" actually means "pursue." It's almost as if David is saying, "Surely the promise—the prediction—is that the Good Shepherd will pursue you with loving-kindness and tender mercy. You can't get away from Him. He'll track you down."

The second prediction is, "I will dwell in the house of the LORD forever." Not only do we have the promise of a quality of life, but we have the prediction of an eternal heavenly residency. We'll be with Him in heaven forever. We will experience the complete absence of all sin, pain, and tears. We will live in a community filled with love and fellowship with other followers of Christ. The Good Shepherd says, "You can bank on these predictions. My predictions always come true."

---

8 How has God pursued you with His love and mercy throughout your life?

How are you experiencing His relentless mercy right now?

PUTTING YOURSELF IN THE PICTURE

GOD PROVIDES

Take time in the coming week to reflect on some of the things God has provided for you. Write them in the space below and take time each day to thank Him for all He provides.

How has God provided for:

- Your physical needs (List the material things He has provided)
- The needs of your heart (List the spiritual blessings he has given you)
- Relationships and community (List the people he has put in your life)

Telling Others About the Shepherd

In this study we discussed what life is like for those who know the Good Shepherd. But there are countless others who don't know Him. Picture one person in your life who does not have a relationship with Jesus. What can you do in the coming days to help that person know the Good Shepherd cares about him or her? Who can pray for you and encourage you as you seek an opportunity to tell this person about the love of the Good Shepherd?

JESUS THE KING

REFLECTIONS FROM SESSION 5

1. If you have taken time since your last meeting to write down some of the things God has provided for you, tell your group about a few of these things. Did reflecting on these develop a thankful heart for the provision of your Good Shepherd?

2. If you took time to tell someone about Jesus, the Good Shepherd, explain how the person responded. In what ways has God begun to transform your heart, giving you a deeper desire to tell others about the Good Shepherd?

THE BIG PICTURE

Many products come with clear warning labels. Here's a little quiz. See if you can identify the products that bear these warnings:

1. Caution: May be harmful if swallowed or may cause severe eye irritation if splashed in eyes. If swallowed, feed milk. If splashed in eyes, flood with water. Call physician immediately. Prolonged contact with metal may cause pitting or discoloration.

2. Danger: Extremely flammable. Harmful or fatal if swallowed.

3. Warning: The surgeon general has determined that [these] are dangerous to your health.

4. Caution: Keep out of reach of children. Harmful if swallowed, inhaled, or absorbed through the skin. Ventilate enclosed areas before returning to the area. Avoid contamination of food and food stuff. Remove pets and birds, and cover fish aquariums before spraying.

5. Caution: Do not use for indoor heating or cooking unless ventilation is provided for exhausting fumes to the outside. Toxic fumes may accumulate and cause death.

(The answers to this quiz are found in the Leader's Notes.)

How did you do on the little quiz? Some of you may take the time to read all the promises and claims that appear in large print all over certain packages. Packagers know how to emphasize the positive qualities of their products, and how to minimize the potential dangers. Usually the warning label is in small print on a back corner of the container. Manufacturers do this so well that few of us are ever really aware, on a conscious level, of the danger in products we purchase.

A WIDE ANGLE VIEW

1

Warning signs all over the place say, "Beware of Dog." "Thin Ice." "Speed reduced to 45 mph ahead." And there are many others. Have you ever missed or ignored a warning sign or label? What were the consequences?

A BIBLICAL PORTRAIT

Read Luke 9:57–62; 14:28–33

2 What kind of warning labels did Jesus post for those who wanted to be His followers?

3 Why do you think Jesus was so painfully clear about what it meant to be His follower?

SHARPENING THE FOCUS

Read Snapshot "Putting It All on the Table"

PUTTING IT ALL ON THE TABLE

It's been my observation that Jesus spent almost as much time warning people to count the cost as He did inviting people into the kingdom. Why did He do that? Jesus put it all on the table so that people could make a decision based on reality. He wanted them to have all of the data and information. He wanted them to know that if He was going to be the King of their life, they would have to relinquish their place on the throne and give it to Him.

Jesus did not want people making a decision based on a slogan, a feeling, or misleading promises. He encouraged people to exercise caution and discretion before they made a commitment to follow.

Jesus also cautioned people about following Him because He wanted to be assured that people were coming to Him on His terms and not their own. Jesus made absolutely no apologies when He asked people to count the cost—to read the package carefully. His promises and His responsibilities appeared equally in bold print. There were no surprises.

Jesus was clear then, and He is just as clear now. He is King of all, or He is not King at all!

4

Respond to the following statements:

"Following Jesus is about receiving, being blessed, being happy, and getting what we really want in life. The beginning and end of the Christian faith is about what we get from God!"

"Following Jesus is about suffering, self-sacrifice, service, and giving. The beginning and end of the Christian faith is about what we give, and give up, for God!"

If you were to take the two strands of thought in the statements above and balance them, what short statement would you make that would complete the following sentence?

Following Jesus is about . . .

Read Snapshot "A New Sensitivity to Sin"

A NEW SENSITIVITY TO SIN

When you follow Jesus as the King, you will develop a new sensitivity to sin. This can complicate your life. Before people become Christians they can live with their own perception of morality. It is easy to create a comfortable combination of your upbringing, your own persuasions, and what is acceptable in the eyes of society. You can find a level of goodness that seems to work for you and feel pretty good about it. But when Christ becomes Lord and King of your life, He calls you to live a holy life. His standards are far above any human standards. He expects transformation. He says, "If you love Me, you will keep every one of My commandments."

5 When you became a follower of Christ, what was one area of sin that God first began dealing with?

How have you experienced His power and help in resisting temptation in this area since then?

How have you struggled at times to avoid this sin?

Read Snapshot "A New Sensitivity to People"

A NEW SENSITIVITY TO PEOPLE

Not only do believers develop a new sensitivity to sin, they develop a new sensitivity to other people and their needs. A workaholic, for example, now says, "I can't be completely consumed by my work and be a godly parent and spouse. Something needs to change in my life so I can love and care for my family." We grow concerned about the people we work with, those who live in our neighborhood, others in the church, and all those we meet in the course of the day.

And not only do we develop a new sensitivity to those who are close to us, but we develop a new sensitivity to people we don't even know. Whereas we used to be able to tune out the needs and problems of other people, now the Holy Spirit moves you to feel for other people and to find ways to show love and concern for them.

6 Choose one area below and discuss how God has changed your heart toward the needs of others in that area since you have become a Christian.

- Toward family members
- Toward friends
- Toward other followers of Christ
- Toward strangers
- Toward your enemies

7 To whom has God sensitized your heart recently?

What do you sense God is prompting you to do in this relationship, and how can your group members encourage you as you follow God's guidance in this relationship?

Read Snapshot "A New Sensitivity to the Holy Spirit"

A NEW SENSITIVITY TO THE HOLY SPIRIT

 When Jesus is King of your life, you also develop a new sensitivity to the leading of the Holy Spirit. He worked in the apostle Peter's life, changing him from a fisherman to a preacher, and he changed the apostle Paul from a Christian persecutor to an evangelist. The Spirit moves guys like Chuck Colson from the oval office in the White House to ministry in maximum security prisons. He took me out of a family produce business and put me into the pastorate. And He's even taken many people out of the pastorate and put them into the marketplace where God wanted them.

If Christ is really Lord and King, we must submit every major decision in our lives to Him. We must never make a major decision without praying to the Holy Spirit and asking for His leading. When you take off on your own and start operating the controls of your own life, the Spirit will begin to tug at your heart and let you know it is time to slow down, to listen to His voice, and to follow His leading.

8
Reflect on a time the Holy Spirit gave you clear direction in your life, or a time He changed the direction in which you were heading. How did you respond?

9
What is one area, decision, or concern in your life at this time with which you need the wisdom and leading of the Holy Spirit?

What role can your small group members play in helping you follow the Spirit's guidance in this area of your life?

LETTING JESUS RULE YOUR RELATIONSHIPS

If Jesus is King of your life, you need to allow Him to lead you in your relationships. Take time in the coming days to pray for Him to take complete charge of the key relationships in your life. Make a list of the significant people in your life in the following areas:

• Your family

• Your church

• Your workplace

• Your neighborhood

• Your friendships

Pray for Jesus to be Lord and ruler of each relationship.

Pray for the Holy Spirit to show you how you can best relate to each person in Christ-honoring ways.

Pray for them to follow Christ as the King of their lives.

LISTENING TO THE SPIRIT

Take five minutes each day for the coming week and quiet your heart to listen to the Holy Spirit. Keep a pen near you and use the space provided below to write down whatever God puts on your heart. It might be the name of a person He wants you to contact, an act of service He wants you to perform, a sin He wants you to confess, or a word of encouragement He wants to speak to you. Simply commit this time to listen for the still, small voice of the Holy Spirit.

LEADER'S NOTES

Leading a Bible discussion—especially for the first time—can make you feel both nervous and excited. If you are nervous, realize that you are in good company. Many biblical leaders, such as Moses, Joshua, and the apostle Paul, felt nervous and inadequate to lead others (see, for example, 1 Cor. 2:3). Yet God's grace was sufficient for them, just as it will be for you.

Some excitement is also natural. Your leadership is a gift to the others in the group. Keep in mind, however, that other group members also share responsibility for the group. Your role is simply to stimulate discussion by asking questions and encouraging people to respond. The suggestions listed below can help you to be an effective leader.

PREPARING TO LEAD

1. Ask God to help you understand and apply the passage to your own life. Unless that happens, you will not be prepared to lead others.
2. Carefully work through each question in the study guide. Meditate and reflect on the passage as you formulate your answers.
3. Familiarize yourself with the Leader's Notes for each session. These will help you understand the purpose of the session and will provide valuable information about the questions in the session. The Leader's Notes are not intended to be read to the group. These notes are primarily for your use as a group leader and for your preparation. However, when you find a section that relates well to your group, you may want to read a brief portion or encourage them to read this section at another time.
4. Pray for the various members of the group. Ask God to use these sessions to make you better disciples of Jesus Christ.
5. Before the first session, make sure each person has a study guide. Encourage them to prepare beforehand for each session.

LEADING THE SESSION

1. Begin the session on time. If people realize that the session begins on schedule, they will work harder to arrive on time.

2. At the beginning of your first time together, explain that these sessions are designed to be discussions, not lectures. Encourage everyone to participate, but realize some may be hesitant to speak during the first few sessions.

3. Don't be afraid of silence. People in the group may need time to think before responding.

4. Avoid answering your own questions. If necessary, rephrase a question until it is clearly understood. Even an eager group will quickly become passive and silent if they think the leader will do most of the talking.

5. Encourage more than one answer to each question. Ask, "What do the rest of you think?" or "Anyone else?" until several people have had a chance to respond.

6. Try to be affirming whenever possible. Let people know you appreciate their insights into the passage.

7. Never reject an answer. If it is clearly wrong, ask, "Which verse led you to that conclusion?" Or let the group handle the problem by asking them what they think about the question.

8. Avoid going off on tangents. If people wander off course, gently bring them back to the passage being considered.

9. Conclude your time together with conversational prayer. Ask God to help you apply those things that you learned in the session.

10. End on time. This will be easier if you control the pace of the discussion by not spending too much time on some questions or too little on others.

We encourage all small group leaders to use *Leading Life-Changing Small Groups* (Zondervan) by Bill Donahue and the Willow Creek Small Group Team while leading their group. Developed and used by Willow Creek Community Church, this guide is an excellent resource for training and equipping followers of Christ to effectively lead small groups. It includes valuable information on how to utilize fun and creative relationship-building exercises for your group; how to plan your meeting; how to share the leadership load by identifying, developing, and working with an "apprentice leader"; and how to find creative ways to do group prayer. In addition, the book includes material and tips on handling potential conflicts and difficult personalities, forming group covenants, inviting new members, improving listening skills, studying the Bible, and much more. Using *Leading Life-Changing Small Groups* will help you create a group that members love to be a part of.

Now let's discuss the different elements of this small group study guide and how to use them for the session portion of your group meeting.

THE BIG PICTURE

Each session will begin with a short story or overview of the lesson theme. This is called "The Big Picture" because it introduces the central theme of the session. You will need to read this section as a group or have group members read it on their own before discussion begins. Here are three ways you can approach this section of the small group session:

- As the group leader, read this section out loud for the whole group and then move into the questions in the next section, "A Wide Angle View." (You might read the first week, but then use the other two options below to encourage group involvement.)
- Ask a group member to volunteer to read this section for the group. This allows another group member to participate. It is best to ask someone in advance to give them time to read over the section before reading it to the group. It is also good to ask someone to volunteer, and not to assign this task. Some people do not feel comfortable reading in front of a group. After a group member has read this section out loud, move into the discussion questions.
- Allow time at the beginning of the session for each person to read this section silently. If you do this, be sure to allow enough time for everyone to finish reading so they can think about what they've read and be ready for meaningful discussion.

A WIDE ANGLE VIEW

This section includes one or more questions that move the group into a general discussion of the session topic. These questions are designed to help group members begin discussing the topic in an open and honest manner. Once the topic of the lesson has been established, move on to the Bible passage for the session.

A BIBLICAL PORTRAIT

This portion of the session includes a Scripture reading and one or more questions that help group members see how the theme of the session is rooted and based in biblical teaching. The Scripture reading can be handled just like "The Big Picture" section: You can read it for the group, have a group member read it, or allow time for silent reading. Make sure everyone has a Bible or that you have Bibles available for those who need them. Once you have read the passage, ask the question(s) in this section so that group members can dig into the truth of the Bible.

SHARPENING THE FOCUS

The majority of the discussion questions for the session are in this section. These questions are practical and help group members apply biblical teaching to their daily lives.

SNAPSHOTS

The "Snapshots" in each session help prepare group members for discussion. These anecdotes give additional insight to the topic being discussed. Each "Snapshot" should be read at a designated point in the session. This is clearly marked in the session as well as in the Leader's Notes. Again, follow the same format as you do with "The Big Picture" section and the "Biblical Portrait" section: Either you read the anecdote, have a group member volunteer to read, or provide time for silent reading. However you approach this section, you will find these anecdotes very helpful in triggering lively dialogue and moving discussion in a meaningful direction.

PUTTING YOURSELF IN THE PICTURE

Here's where you roll up your sleeves and put the truth into action. This portion is very practical and action-oriented. At the end of each session there will be suggestions for one or two ways group members can put what they've just learned into practice. Review the action goals at the end of each session and challenge group members to work on one or more of them in the coming week.

You will find follow-up questions for the "Putting Yourself in the Picture" section at the beginning of the next week's session. Starting with the second week, there will be time set aside at the beginning of the session to look back and talk about how you have tried to apply God's Word in your life since your last time together.

PRAYER

You will want to open and close your small group with a time of prayer. Occasionally, there will be specific direction within a session for how you can do this. Most of the time, however, you will need to decide the best place to stop and pray. You may want to pray or have a group member volunteer to begin the lesson with a prayer. Or you might want to read "The Big Picture" and discuss the "Wide Angle View" questions before opening in prayer. In some cases, it might be best to open in prayer after you have read the Bible passage. You need to decide where you feel an opening prayer best fits for your group.

When opening in prayer, think in terms of the session theme and pray for group members (including yourself) to be responsive to the truth of Scripture and the working of the Holy Spirit. If you have seekers in your group (people investigating Christianity but not yet believers), be sensitive to your expectations for group prayer. Seekers may not yet be ready to take part in group prayer.

Be sure to close your group with a time of prayer as well. One option is for you to pray for the entire group. Or you might allow time for group members to offer audible prayers that others can agree with in their hearts. Another approach would be to allow a time of silence for one-on-one prayers with God and then to close this time with a simple "Amen."

JESUS THE MAN

PHILIPPIANS 2:5—11

INTRODUCTION

In this session group members will learn that their Savior is more than just a friend. We have a sympathetic Savior. Sometimes when we face the difficulties of life we want to say, "No one understands!" This is not entirely true. Though the people around us may not understand, we need to learn to say, "No one understands like Jesus!" He has experienced all we experience, but He has remained sinless. He has faced the challenges of human relationships, the burdens of daily labor, and the pain and suffering that are part of every life. And not only does He understand, He cares!

THE BIG PICTURE

Take time to read this introduction with the group. There are suggestions for how this can be done in the beginning of the leader's section.

A WIDE ANGLE VIEW

Question One We have all had times when we have felt very alone, as if no one could possibly understand what we were going through. Take time for group members to communicate their stories and how Jesus walked with them through their pain and struggle. In addition to the story in the session from my own life, you may want to relate another example that comes from the life experience of my wife, Lynne.

Early in our marriage Lynne had two rather traumatic miscarriages. During the hours, days, and weeks after she miscarried (one time with a set of twins), I just came right out and said, "Lynne, you know me. You know I love you, and you know I really can't understand what you're going through. I can help around the house with the chores. I can hang around outside your door or come in and sit by the bed. I can stay out of your way if you need some space. I love you, and I'll be here for you." Lynne did need me to be with her. However, she did not expect me to understand how she was feeling, and I did not pretend I did. You see, we can care even when we don't completely understand.

A BIBLICAL PORTRAIT

Read Philippians 2:5–11

Questions Two & Three This passage is one of the most powerful reminders of what Jesus gave up and suffered because of His love for lost people. If you want to see that lost people matter to God, just read this passage and try to get your mind around all Jesus did for us when He left the glory of heaven to be born in an obscure manger, live on a sin-plagued earth, and die on a rugged cross.

Allow time for group members to reflect on not only what Jesus did, but also what He suffered for them. Encourage group members to express how this makes them feel. How much love did it take for God to send His only Son to suffer this way for us?

SHARPENING THE FOCUS

Read Snapshot "Jesus Understands Relationships" before Question 4

Questions Four & Five In 1 Peter 5:7 it is as if Peter is saying, "Go ahead. God understands. Go to Him in prayer and solitude. Close the door of your room, open the door of your heart, and pour it out to God. Cast all your cares, anxieties, and frustrations on Him. He really cares." In a spirit of humility and dependence, we are invited to pour out our hearts to God. Until we try it, we will never know how much healing this can bring.

The only way I weathered the grief of losing my dad so abruptly was by realizing that Jesus understood all about grief and pain. I went to Him and poured my heart out. And somehow, some way, He touched me. He consoled me on a level of which people were incapable of consoling me. This also worked for Lynne as she grieved the pain and loss of her miscarriages. Somehow, when we seek Christ there is a healing, a mending, a quieting that can't be found anywhere else. When we turn to Him, we experience a refueling and refocusing that only He can bring.

Do the problems go away? Most of the time, no. But the perspective of your mind and your attitude toward the problems change. When you know that somebody understands, cares, and can touch you, your outlook can begin to change.

Read Snapshot "Jesus Understands Work" before Question 6

Question Six Can you see God's wisdom in having Jesus spend most of His life in the marketplace? Because of this, He understands our daily labors.

Some of us are in the formal marketplace and others work in the home, but all of us spend a great deal of time doing our daily work and fulfilling our vocation. That's where most of us find ourselves getting exhausted mentally and physically, frustrated by pressures and disappointments. And that's where many of us are most apt to cry out, "No one understands what I'm going through."

When are we going to let Jesus help us in the marketplace, in our homes, in our daily work? When are we going to cut the Lone Ranger act? We need to allow the sympathetic Savior to stand alongside of us in the workplace. We need to go to Him in the middle of the workday in solitude and humility and pour our hearts out to Him over our daily concerns. Thank God Jesus was a carpenter. He understands our daily labors.

Read Snapshot "Jesus Understands Pain and Suffering" before Question 7

Questions Seven & Eight Many of your small group members, if not all, are well-acquainted with ridicule because of their vocation, mailing address, personal background, handicap, or one of countless other reasons. There are also those who carry physical pain in their body day by day. It hurts to walk, to lie down, to stand up. In these situations it's so easy to say no one understands. But Jesus does.

Some in your group may have suffered rejection from their families. Those who have been deserted, those whose spouses have been unfaithful, those who have gone through the pain and agony of separation and divorce are some of the most brokenhearted people I know. Others in your group might feel rejection because of loss of employment. Jesus knows about rejection. He understands.

Despite ridicule, rejection, and pain, we have to hold onto this truth: We have a sympathetic Savior who understands us when no one else can. We must learn to turn to Him for comfort when no one else can meet our needs.

PUTTING YOURSELF IN THE PICTURE

Tell group members you will be providing time at the beginning of the next meeting for them to discuss how they have put their faith into action. Let them tell their stories. However, don't limit their interaction to the two options provided.

They may have put themselves into the picture in some other way as a result of your study. Allow for honest and open communication.

Also, be clear that there will not be any kind of a "test" or forced reporting. All you are going to do is allow time for people to volunteer to talk about how they have applied what they learned in your last study. Some group members will feel pressured if they think you are going to make everyone provide a "report." You don't want anyone to skip the next group because they are afraid of having to say they did not follow up on what they learned from the prior session. Focus instead on providing a place for honest communication without creating pressure and fear of being embarrassed.

Every session from this point on will open with a look back at the "Putting Yourself in the Picture" section of the previous session.

JESUS THE TEACHER

MATTHEW 5:3–12; 6:5–15; 7:24–27

INTRODUCTION

Jesus was a master teacher. Although people debate some aspects of who Jesus was, this seems to be one of the central areas of common ground. We all agree that Jesus was a powerful and effective teacher and communicator. He taught with authority through graphic images, and He called people to action. In this session we will think about the teaching ministry of Jesus and seek to grow as followers of Christ who hear His voice and follow His teaching.

THE BIG PICTURE

Take time to read this introduction with the group. There are suggestions for how this can be done in the beginning of the leader's section.

A BIBLICAL PORTRAIT

Read Matthew 5:3–12; 6:5–15; 7:24–27

Questions Two & Three These three passages are taken from the Sermon on the Mount. They are examples of Jesus' teaching, which was authoritative, graphic, and practical. As you study these passages, look at two main themes: first, the message Jesus is communicating and how it touches the heart and life of a follower of Christ; and second, how Jesus communicated that message.

SHARPENING THE FOCUS

Read Snapshot "Jesus Taught with Authority" before Question 4

Question Four Often Jesus would begin His teaching with the phrase, "Verily, verily, I say unto you" or "Truly, truly, I say unto you." Jesus was saying, "This is the end of all discussions on what I'm about ready to talk about." People could not hear a sermon from Jesus without walking away feeling as though they had heard a word from God Himself. And in fact, they had. That was the key to Jesus' authority: He was God in the flesh. In John 14:6, Jesus said, "I am the way and the truth and the life." In other words, whenever Jesus opened His mouth, only truth was spoken.

Read Snapshot "Jesus Taught Graphically" before Question 6

Questions Six & Seven Jesus painted His messages with pictures, and these pictures speak to us louder than words. The story of the camel and the eye of the needle is one of my favorites. One day Jesus said to His listeners, "Bring a camel to the screen of your imagination. Got it? Hang on to that picture. Now think of a needle. All right, now try to walk the camel through the eye of that needle."

I can just hear the crowd laughing or staring in confusion. They must have been thinking, *Jesus, what are you saying? You can't walk a camel through the eye of a needle!* Then Jesus really rocked their world by saying, "Well, I'll tell you what. The odds of a rich man getting into heaven are about the same odds as your camel walking through the eye of your needle." Every wealthy person in that crowd must have gulped.

Jesus was saying, "Look. Rich people have a tendency to be self-sufficient and self-reliant. In order for a person to enter the kingdom of heaven, that person has to be humble. He has to rely on the work of another person." This work was the work of Jesus Christ on the cross. In order for a person to enter the kingdom of heaven, a person has to be repentant over his sin. He has to be meek. He has to be teachable. And Jesus says, "That's a very difficult thing for rich men."

Something supernatural has to happen to make a camel shrink small enough to fit through the eye of a needle. In the same way, something supernatural has to happen to a rich man to get him into heaven.

Read Snapshot "Jesus Taught Practically" before Question 8

Questions Eight & Nine No wonder the multitudes followed Jesus around to hear Him speak—His teaching changed lives. He called people to radical commitment and dramatic action. After people heard Jesus, they were never the same. Allow your group members some time to tell about how their lives have been changed by hearing and following the practical teaching of Jesus.

Jesus answered life's most complex questions:

"Here's where you came from—you've been created in the image of a personal God."

"Here's what you are—a marred image of that Creator. You're a sinner."

"Here's what you need—a loving, sympathetic Savior to cleanse you from your sin."

"Here's what lies beyond the grave—resurrection for both the righteous and the wicked."

"Here's how you get to heaven—through trusting in Me, Jesus Christ."

"Here's how you get to hell—by rebelling against God or ignoring Him."

"Here's how you make your life count in the meantime—by seeking first the kingdom of God."

Here's how to act in the marketplace . . . Here's how to build a church . . . Here's how to build a marriage . . . Here's how to build a family . . . Here's how to build relationships. Jesus laid it out principle by principle. He said, "There is no great mystery about these things. Even children can understand them." And at the end of the Sermon on the Mount Jesus said, "If you've heard my teachings and have no plans to act on them, then you are as foolish as a man who builds a great big house on a patch of quicksand." His invitation was clear: "Build your lives on My words, and you will be standing on solid rock!" He was the master teacher. As followers of Christ, we must learn to hear His words and follow them.

PUTTING YOURSELF IN THE PICTURE

Challenge group members to take time in the coming week to use part or all of this application section as an opportunity for continued growth.

JESUS THE PHYSICIAN

LUKE 5:12—16

INTRODUCTION

This session's subject is one of the most hotly debated subjects in Christendom. The whole topic of healing has brought about much confusion. We read newspaper advertisements about healers coming to town. When we look through the *TV Guide,* we easily find programming featuring healers. Are healers for real? Are some, or all, of them phoney? How can we tell?

If we are going to have a biblical perspective on healing, we must first look at the Master Healer—the Great Physician. In Jesus' healing ministry we see Him as gentle, personal, sensitive, and caring. He came alongside ailing and broken people and touched their lives.

In this session we will look at some of the false views of healing that exist in the church today. We will also look at the biblical teaching on this highly controversial topic.

THE BIG PICTURE

Take time to read this introduction with the group. There are suggestions for how this can be done in the beginning of the leader's section.

A WIDE ANGLE VIEW

Question One This is a real-life story that will evoke a response from everyone in your group. Sadly, this is not an isolated incident. There are many such stories and groups that still teach this view of "divine healing." Allow group members to express how they react to this story. Use the story as a starting point for understanding how God wants us to view divine healing. Be careful to draw insights about their views as well as about their past experiences with healings.

A BIBLICAL PORTRAIT

Read Luke 5:12–16

Question Two If you read this passage too quickly, you might be tempted to say, "I understand exactly what's going on here." But look a little closer. Read between the lines and try to understand what's really going on. Catch the drama of Jesus, the Great Physician.

Here is a man with the deadly disease of leprosy. Leprosy was a horrible disease in Jesus' day and it still ravages lives today. I have seen leprosy firsthand in Kenya, Uganda, and a few other cities in eastern Africa. When this devastating disease attacks a body, people lose fingers, limbs, sometimes even parts of the face fall off. I once saw a beggar whose leprosy had taken his arm up to his elbow. He balanced a little tin cup on what was left of his upper arm and kept calling out, "Penny, penny, penny."

In Jesus' day there was a social stigma attached to leprosy. People feared it was contagious, so the people who had this disease were alienated from society and had to live in separate communities with others who also had the disease. If anyone came near, they had to shout out, "Stay away! Unclean! Unclean!"

With this background in mind, picture the man in the story running right up to Jesus, falling flat on his face, and crying out, "I'm giving You honor. I don't know what You're going to do, but You're my only hope. I'm pouring out my heart before You. I'm on my face in the dirt." Then he said, "Lord, I have no doubt about Your power. Your reputation has preceded You. But Lord, would You look kindly on someone like *me*? If You are willing, I know You can heal me."

Then Jesus reached down to pick up the man and look at him eye to eye. These actions were unconventional and unnecessary—Jesus could certainly have relieved this man's illness by His spoken word alone—but He chose to bring about healing by touching him. Jesus simply reached out and healed this man in his need.

Question Three If you ever undertake a serious study of the healings of Jesus, you'll probably come to a few basic conclusions. First, Jesus' healing ministry was second only to His teaching ministry, and often He appeared to value the two ministries equally. Jesus was every bit as concerned about the body as the soul of a person. Second, Jesus' compassion is more evident in His healing ministry than anywhere else. Love, concern, and compassion pour from the recorded episodes of healings in the Gospels.

Third, Jesus healed for the sake of the afflicted, not for the applause of onlookers. In other episodes you will read this little phrase, "and Jesus took the person off to the side." What's going on here? What does Jesus do for a person who has already been humiliated and embarrassed because of a debilitating disease or illness? He says, "I know there may be thousands of people gathered, but I want everybody to sit tight and wait a few minutes," and then He takes that one person and goes off to the side so He can minister to them without turning them into a spectacle.

Fourth, Jesus' healing was personalized. Sometimes when people wanted to be healed, Jesus would begin the conversation by saying, "Well, first, what is your name?" He made it clear that He cared about people and wanted to be personal in His ministry to those who were hurting.

And fifth, when credit was given, it was always directed heavenward. Jesus would often say, "Now go glorify My Father, who is in heaven. Go and tell other people how My Father has had mercy on you." The miracles validated Jesus' claims, but were not meant to make Him popular.

SHARPENING THE FOCUS

Read Snapshot "Beware of Sensationalists" before Question 4

Question Four Many sick and afflicted people are desperate for a cure. They'll watch almost anything, support almost anyone, and overlook almost any contrary evidence in hopes of getting healed. In recent years we have heard of many of these "healers" who are living double lives and who have been caught in financial—or any other—impropriety. However, they still seem to multiply and go on with their healing shows.

What hurts me so much is that all of this seems to be happening at the expense of people who are afflicted and who are desperately searching and longing for healing. I am concerned that the sensationalists are going to become even more prevalent in the coming years. We need to be on guard.

Read Snapshot "Beware of Confessionalists" before Question 5

Question Five Is healing always directly related to the amount of a person's faith? I don't buy that notion. If this were true, then Paul, one of the most outstanding personalities in

Christian history, must not have had enough faith! Paul prayed for healing and God told him, "My grace is sufficient." However, even though Paul healed other people, he himself did not experience physical healing in this lifetime.

Is it honest to go around saying, "I have been healed. I have been healed," when you know you haven't been healed? Some years ago I did a radio talk show and someone called in and said, "I have a crippling illness and for the past six months I've been going to see faith healers who tell me I am already healed even though my body is still crippled. I can't live with myself anymore because I know I am lying to myself, to others, and to God." He said, "My friends and my family members know better, and I'm losing my dignity by pretending I am healed when I am not."

Confessionalists are manipulative. They say, "Claim it in faith and God must do it." They obligate God to bring healing. I don't know about you, but I don't obligate God to do anything. I say, "God, if by Your grace You want to give me another day of life, that's Your business. And if You choose to give me another day, I know it is only by Your great grace."

Confessionalists also try to convince people that they have to buy more tapes, attend more meetings, and give more money so they can build their faith. It becomes a circular system that afflicted people get sucked into. People trapped in this teaching soon discover that they can never listen to enough messages, attend enough meetings, give enough money, or do enough works of kindness. Finally, they end up defeated.

Nowhere in Scripture are we told that the amount or intensity of our faith determines the extent of our healing. Faith is involved in the healing process, but there is no guarantee attached to it. Because God is sovereign and always has the last word, ultimately we must trust in His wisdom rather than our own faith.

Read Snapshot "A Balanced View of Healing" before Question 7

Questions Seven & Eight Many of us have personally experienced supernatural healing without giving God an ounce of credit for it. God still heals today, and He occasionally uses what we would refer to as the natural process of healing. But this natural process is nonetheless miraculous. Some years ago my son Todd fell off a chair and took a swan dive right into the fireplace. He ended up with an ugly gash on his cheek. After the bleeding stopped I brought him to the mirror and said, "Hey listen, buddy, Jesus is going to heal that. In just a few months, that cheek is going to look just like the other cheek." I don't think he believed me, but I would bring him to the mirror every four or five days and show him the healing process. Finally, one day I said, "Which cheek was it, buddy?" He said, "I don't know which cheek it was." And I said, "Because Jesus healed it so well, it's just like the other one. It's a miracle." This is natural healing, but it is still from the hand of God. We need to learn how to give God glory when He chooses to heal through the regenerative system built into our bodies.

God also chooses to heal through the hands and the skill of doctors. Luke, who wrote the books of Luke and Acts, was a physician. There is nothing in Scripture that would prohibit us from going to doctors. The Bible applauds the gaining of wisdom and the discovery of new insights. One of the most frequent ways God chooses to heal today is through medical means. Because of medical advances that God has graciously allowed, polio, tuberculosis, and other epidemics are almost nonexistent today. We need to give Him praise for giving us minds that can study, experiment, and eventually find treatments for serious diseases.

Finally, God sometimes chooses to heal through a supernatural touch of His hand. In our church we gather every month to pray for healing. We have had some exciting things happen. We have seen women who could not conceive have children. We have seen an autistic child who was totally out of control experience dramatic improvement so that he was able to be put in a special program at school because he was advancing and adjusting so well. I could go on and on about the miracles God has done. We need to pray in faith for healing and accept God's answer. When He works miracles, we need to be sure to give Him all the praise!

PUTTING YOURSELF IN THE PICTURE

Challenge group members to take time in the coming week to use part or all of this application section as an opportunity for continued growth.

JESUS
THE SERVANT

JOHN 13:1—17

INTRODUCTION

If any character trait binds the human race together, it would be self-centeredness. Without the power of the Holy Spirit changing our hearts, our natural tendency is to think primarily about ourselves. Many marriages disintegrate because one of the partners simply says, "She doesn't turn me on any more" or "He doesn't do anything for me any more." Many friendships fall apart because people fail to invest the time and energy it takes to build strong relationships.

In this session we will hear Jesus calling us to follow His example of serving. This is a great challenge in a selfish world, but when we look at Jesus as our example and seek the power of the Holy Spirit, we can learn to become the servants He wants us to be.

THE BIG PICTURE

Take time to read this introduction with the group. There are suggestions for how this can be done in the beginning of the leader's section.

A WIDE ANGLE VIEW

Question One Many of us want "three dollars worth of God" in a paper sack that can be opened up and used at our disposal and for our convenience. We acknowledge that God doesn't come in three dollar packages, but if the truth be known, we would like it if He did. Jesus made the Christian faith an active faith when He told us we are supposed to spend our lives following His example of servanthood. He committed Himself to thinking of others, to meeting their needs and serving them. Then He told us to do the same. This means we can't get away with a three-dollar portion of God; we need all of Him. Or to put it another way, He wants all of us!

A BIBLICAL PORTRAIT

Read John 13:1–17

Questions Two & Three Jesus didn't just teach the principles of servanthood, He modeled them. In this passage Jesus washes the feet of the disciples. That's a strange thing for us to be talking about in our day, but back then there were very few paved roads. Walking from place to place in sandals, your feet would get very dirty. If you went into someone's house, you would want to have your feet cleaned.

The custom of the day was for the owner of the house to provide someone to wash the feet of any visitors. If someone was wealthy enough, they would have a slave standing at the door who would help guests out of their sandals, wash their feet, dry them, clean their sandals, and place them by the door. Guests would eat barefoot, and then pick up their clean sandals as they left.

If the family was not wealthy enough to hire a servant, then it was an understood cultural custom that one of the first guests to arrive would volunteer to wash feet on behalf of the host, who was usually busy fixing food, setting the table, and greeting the guests. In this passage the disciples gathered together in the Upper Room for the Last Supper. There was no formal host, so as the individual disciples arrived, each could have and should have offered to wash the feet of the others as they entered the room. Instead, we read that they all just sat down for the meal, reclining at the table. None of them offered to serve the others. Seeing this, Jesus got up from the supper table, got a towel and a basin of water, and began washing their feet. He was the only one willing to serve the others!

As Jesus washed the feet of each of His followers—even the feet of Judas, who was just hours away from betraying Him—Peter protested momentarily. But Jesus said, "You call me 'Teacher' and 'Lord,' and rightly so, for that is what I am. Now that I, your Lord and Teacher, have washed your feet, you also should wash one another's feet. I have set you an example that you should do as I have done for you. I tell you the truth, no servant is greater than his master, nor is a messenger greater than the one who sent him. Now that you know these things, you will be blessed if you do them" (John 13:13–17). Interestingly, Jesus didn't say, "Now I have washed your feet, so you wash Mine." Jesus said, "Wash one another's feet."

SHARPENING THE FOCUS

Read Snapshot "Me-ism" before Question 4

Questions Four & Five We live in a "me" saturated culture. Allow group members to tell about how they see this problem in the world around them. The next part is more difficult. Take time for group members to be honest about where the monster of me-ism has dug its claws into their lives. Where are they fighting battles of selfishness? This is vulnerable ground, and you may want to pause for prayer before you open the door for communicating on this deep level.

Read Snapshot "Jesus the Servant" before Question 6

Questions Six & Seven In Mark 9:33 the disciples and Jesus came to a town called Capernaum on the north side of the sea of Galilee. When He was in the house, Jesus began to question the disciples, asking them, "What were you arguing about on the road?" Apparently some of the disciples had lingered behind the group and were discussing something pretty intensely. It turned out that they were discussing which one of them was the greatest! Jesus then called them together and said to them, "If anyone wants to be first, he must be the very last, and the servant of all." In order to be great in the eyes of God, you have to be a servant.

This is one of many examples of Jesus teaching or modeling servanthood. Allow time for group members to recall stories of Jesus serving others. This will continue to set the scene for what needs to happen in all of our hearts.

Read Snapshot "A Call to Service" before Question 8

Questions Eight & Nine The lack of the spirit of graciousness conveys the absence of a servantlike spirit. A true servant has that spirit of graciousness. He or she looks at life's situations and says, "How can I help out? What can I do for this person that will model the love and concern of Jesus?"

True servants also manifest a spirit of helpfulness. This helpfulness can be seen in loaning a vehicle to someone in need, sharing meals, even giving away money to those who need it. True servants find themselves saying, "What can I do to help?" And we know that God, who sees the things done in secret, will reward every anonymous deed done for God's glory. Don't ever think that just because no one's watching, the deed is unseen. Your Father in heaven doesn't miss a single one.

A servant also has a desire to be useful. True servants want to be used by God and others. They love serving; it energizes them. It's the key to the fulfillment they have been looking for. True servants often kneel in prayer and say, "Oh God, how can I serve You more?" They go to other followers of Christ and say, "How can I be of help to you? Do you need anything? How can I serve you more?" This is the heart of Jesus, and this is the heart of a servant.

PUTTING YOURSELF IN THE PICTURE

Challenge group members to take time in the coming week to use part or all of this application section as an opportunity for continued growth.

JESUS THE SHEPHERD

PSALM 23

INTRODUCTION

In this session we will reflect on Psalm 23, the Shepherd's Psalm. The six power-packed verses in this psalm give us great insight into Jesus as our Shepherd. I like to divide this psalm into three sections: first, "What the Shepherd Provides"; second, "How the Shepherd Protects"; and third, "What the Shepherd Predicts." The bottom line is that we all need the Good Shepherd. The question is, will we receive and follow Him?

This psalm loses all of its punch without the personal, "The Lord is *my* Shepherd." It will be important to ask this simple question at the beginning of your small group: "Is the Lord *your* Shepherd?" The Good Shepherd, who laid down His life for the sheep, wants to lead and guide each person in your small group. Pray for all hearts, including your own, to be open to God's leading.

THE BIG PICTURE

Take time to read this introduction with the group. There are suggestions for how this can be done in the beginning of the leader's section.

A BIBLICAL PORTRAIT

Read Psalm 23

Questions Two & Three Because this psalm is so familiar, the responses to question two should be fairly clear. You will find some group members may be so familiar with this psalm that they know its words by memory.

Question three, however, will give a whole new look at the psalm. You see, we often want to act as if this psalm applies to everyone. In fact, it does not. Only those who have accepted the Good Shepherd and committed to follow Jesus can experience the truth of this psalm. If someone has not experienced the forgiveness of sins through Jesus, they don't know Him as their Shepherd.

When you take each statement in this psalm and say, "If the Lord is *not* my Shepherd, then I will *not* . . .," the psalm takes on a whole new meaning. Two things happen. First, we realize what we have gained through the Shepherd. Not only have we been saved *to* something, we have been saved *from* something. Reading the psalm this way will make this painfully clear. And second, we will begin to look at seekers and those who are running from God in a whole different way. They are people who do not have a Good Shepherd or any of the promises made in this psalm. Knowing this, we are compelled to pray for them and do all we can to let them know about the Good Shepherd's love.

Sharpening the Focus

Read Snapshot "How the Shepherd Provides" before Question 4

Questions Four & Five When King David wrote this psalm, he could have called God anything. He could have called Him King, Ruler, Rock, Fortress, Deliverer, the Transcendent One. But for good reason, in this most sensitive psalm, David says, "The Lord is my Shepherd."

David begins, "Because the Lord is my Shepherd, I have everything that I need." The first thing the Shepherd provides for you if you'll open up your heart and receive it is a spirit of *contentment*. As followers of Christ we don't have to keep trying to fill our voids the way we did before we came to Christ. We don't have to drink our emptiness away, or party it away, or buy it away. No more frenzied activity. No more fantasies that one more possession, trip, or thrill will heal the gnawing in our heart. All these are ancient history for those who know the Shepherd.

The picture of contentment is seen in the words, "He makes me lie down in green pastures, he leads me beside quiet waters." Sheep lying down. More than enough grass for grazing. Plenty of clear, cool, refreshing water from which to drink. The flock is content. It has everything it needs.

The Shepherd also provides *restoration* for the soul. How many times has your soul been ravaged? Some of your group members could say, "Just this past year my spouse left me" or "I got my pink slip at work after fifteen years of service" or "I've been let down by my closest friends." And the list could go on and on. If you took time as a group, you could probably uncover hardship after hardship, disaster after disaster, blow after blow. In the face of those kinds of difficulties, the Good Shepherd promises to restore our soul. And He promises to do it carefully, tenderly, and completely.

The third gift from the Shepherd is *guidance*. "He leads me," the psalm says. "He guides me in His paths." Often it seems that catastrophe and confusion go hand-in-hand. When people are reeling from the harsh realities of tragedy or loss, the common result is often confusion. In times of pain and loss, the compass is spinning wildly and familiar landmarks are obscured. This psalm gives us a quiet assurance that the Shepherd will provide guidance. He'll be our landmark. He'll set our compass straight and will give us definite direction, either through His Word, through advice and encouragement from other Christians, or directly through the power of the Holy Spirit.

Before the next question, you may want to pause as a group to lift up prayers for those who have communicated a specific need in their life at this time. Ask Jesus, the Good Shepherd, to meet these needs.

Read Snapshot "How the Shepherd Protects" before Question 6

Questions Six & Seven David was a warrior. He knew what it was like to hear swords clashing in battle, to have arrows whizzing by his head, to have his troops dying at his side. He knew what it was like to have everything look dark and to feel as if he was just moments away from destruction. But still he says, "I know what it feels like to have the Good Shepherd protect and preserve me. He has been with me in the midst of battle. It feels like God actually prepares a table and sets out a seven-course dinner, right in the middle of the war."

Jesus wants to do the same thing for us. He does not promise all of the battles and storms of life will disappear, but He does promise to protect us in the middle of it all. The Shepherd says, "I'm going to wrap My arms around you and protect you. I want you to feel safe inside My protection. I'm going to prepare a table for you in the middle of the battle. I'm going to make your cup overflow." Do you realize what that means? It means we can have joy, fullness in our spirits, and worship spilling over from our hearts, even when it seems everything is caving in around us.

Again, you may want to pause to pray specifically for those who have expressed an area of their lives in which they need the protection of the Shepherd. Be sure to encourage group members to continue praying for these needs in the days to come.

Read Snapshot "What the Shepherd Predicts" before Question 8

Question Eight Unbelievers want to hide from God because they feel as if God is tracking them down. In a very real sense, they are right. God *is* tracking them down. As a Good Shepherd, He wants them to come into the fold. For those who have already entered into a relationship with God through Christ, God is still tracking us down. He's pursuing us with His loving-kindness and tender mercy.

Ten years ago I thought God was simply gracious and loving. Five years ago I was embarrassed at how ridiculous my appraisal was five years prior to that. Every year that passes I find myself increasingly humbled and almost embarrassed by God's incredible loving-kindness and tender mercy toward me, no matter what I go through. The same will be true for you.

PUTTING YOURSELF IN THE PICTURE

Challenge group members to take time in the coming week to use part or all of this application section as an opportunity for continued growth.

JESUS THE KING
LUKE 9:57–62 AND 14:28–33

INTRODUCTION

We've already learned about Jesus the Man, the Teacher, the Physician, the Servant, and the Good Shepherd. In this final session we are focusing on the concept of Jesus as the King. The theme of Jesus' kingship centers on His complete leadership and rule in our lives. Contrary to modern packaging methods, Jesus never tried to hide the potential dangers of following Him. He didn't sway multitudes by promising health, wealth, and happiness, and then whispering quietly, "Oh, incidentally, there may be a few responsibilities or sacrifices now and then." On the contrary, Jesus was so up front about the dangers and difficulties involved in Christianity that sometimes we read statements like, "And after hearing this, many withdrew from Him and decided not to walk with Him anymore." Jesus laid it all out on the table when he called people to follow Him as the King and ruler of their lives. This is the same way He calls people today: No surprises and no small print.

THE BIG PICTURE

Take time to read this introduction with the group. There are suggestions for how this can be done in the beginning of the leader's section.

Answers to the Quiz
  1. Bleach
  2. A gasoline can
  3. Cigarettes
  4. Insect killer
  5. Charcoal

A BIBLICAL PORTRAIT

Read Luke 9:57–62; 14:28–33

Questions Two & Three Jesus urged those who are contemplating following Him to "Count the cost." To illustrate this He said, "If a man is going to build a house, he needs to

get estimates. He must know what it's going to cost him."
Jesus knew that the ultimate embarrassment was to get
halfway through a building project and not be able to finish
because you didn't count the cost up front. He also used an
illustration of a king going out to battle, saying that the king
better have an idea of how strong the enemy was and how
strong his own troops were, or he might just risk everyone's
life. Jesus frequently reminded people that before they made a
commitment to Him, they had better know what He expected of them. What did He expect? Everything! Total allegiance.
Jesus let people know His desire was to be the sovereign ruler
and King of their lives.

Sharpening the Focus

**Read Snapshot "Putting It All on the Table" before
Question 4**

**Read Snapshot "A New Sensitivity to Sin" before
Question 5**

Question Five This question may make some people feel
vulnerable. You may want to let your group know that this is
a safe place where they can open up their lives and be loved.
Below is an example of the type of story they might want to
relate.

Some years ago I had an opportunity to go motorcycle riding
with some friends. We had an extra motorcycle so I called one
of our staff members who loves riding motorcycles and invited him to come along. I knew he wanted to go, and I knew he
had the day open, so I was pretty sure he would say yes. I was
surprised when he said he could not come with us. When I
asked him why, he said, "My motorcycle license has expired
and I know God's Word says to obey the governing authorities." Both of us knew there was very little chance his license
would ever be checked, but God had made his heart sensitive
to sin and he was not going to risk disobeying God.

**Read Snapshot "A New Sensitivity to People" before
Question 6**

Questions Six & Seven When we follow Jesus as our King,
our view of others changes dramatically. Over time we begin
to care about those who lack the basic needs of life. We want
to do what we can to help those in need. We begin to be sensitive to racism in ourselves or others. Our hearts are softened
and we desire to show love and care to our family members,
friends, fellow Christians, and even to strangers and our ene-

mies. When Jesus is on the throne, our heart begins to beat with His heart and we can never be the same.

Take time for your group to talk about how God has been changing their hearts. Remember, this change is usually a process and can be either dramatic or very ordinary. No matter what the change, it is a result of the power of Jesus as He rules and guides our lives.

PUTTING YOURSELF IN THE PICTURE

Challenge group members to take time in the coming week to use part or all of this application section as an opportunity for continued growth.

ADDITIONAL WILLOW CREEK RESOURCES

Small Group Resources

Coaching Life-Changing Small Group Leaders, by Bill Donahue and Greg Bowman
The Complete Book of Questions, by Garry Poole
The Connecting Church, by Randy Frazee
Leading Life-Changing Small Groups, by Bill Donahue and the Willow Creek Team
The Seven Deadly Sins of Small Group Ministry, by Bill Donahue and Russ Robinson
Walking the Small Group Tightrope, by Bill Donahue and Russ Robinson

Evangelism Resources

Becoming a Contagious Christian (book), by Bill Hybels and Mark Mittelberg
The Case for a Creator, by Lee Strobel
The Case for Christ, by Lee Strobel
The Case for Faith, by Lee Strobel
Seeker Small Groups, by Garry Poole
The Three Habits of Highly Contagious Christians, by Garry Poole

Spiritual Gifts and Ministry

Network Revised (training course), by Bruce Bugbee and Don Cousins
The Volunteer Revolution, by Bill Hybels
What You Do Best in the Body of Christ—Revised, by Bruce Bugbee

Marriage and Parenting

Fit to Be Tied, by Bill and Lynne Hybels
Surviving a Spiritual Mismatch in Marriage, by Lee and Leslie Strobel

Ministry Resources

An Hour on Sunday, by Nancy Beach
Building a Church of Small Groups, by Bill Donahue and Russ Robinson
The Heart of the Artist, by Rory Noland
Making Your Children's Ministry the Best Hour of Every Kid's Week, by Sue Miller and
    David Staal
Thriving as an Artist in the Church, by Rory Noland

Curriculum

An Ordinary Day with Jesus, by John Ortberg and Ruth Haley Barton
Becoming a Contagious Christian (kit), by Mark Mittelberg, Lee Strobel, and Bill Hybels
Good Sense Budget Course, by Dick Towner, John Tofilon, and the Willow Creek Team
If You Want to Walk on Water, You've Got to Get Out of the Boat, by John Ortberg with
    Stephen and Amanda Sorenson
The Life You've Always Wanted, by John Ortberg with Stephen and Amanda Sorenson
The Old Testament Challenge, by John Ortberg with Kevin and Sherry Harney, Mindy
    Caliguire, and Judson Poling

WILLOW
Willow Creek Association

Willow Creek Association
Vision, Training, Resources for Prevailing Churches

This resource was created to serve you and to help you build a local church that prevails. It is just one of many ministry tools that are part of the Willow Creek Resources® line, published by the Willow Creek Association together with Zondervan.

The Willow Creek Association (WCA) was created in 1992 to serve a rapidly growing number of churches from across the denominational spectrum that are committed to helping unchurched people become fully devoted followers of Christ. Membership in the WCA now numbers over 10,500 Member Churches worldwide from more than ninety denominations.

The Willow Creek Association links like-minded Christian leaders with each other and with strategic vision, training, and resources in order to help them build prevailing churches designed to reach their redemptive potential. Here are some of the ways the WCA does that.

- **A2: Building Prevailing Acts 2 Churches—Today**—an annual two-and-a-half day event, held at Willow Creek Community Church in South Barrington, Illinois, to explore strategies for building churches that reach out to seekers and build believers, and to discover new innovations and breakthroughs from Acts 2 churches around the country.

- **The Leadership Summit**—a once a year, two-and-a-half-day conference to envision and equip Christians with leadership gifts and responsibilities. Presented live at Willow Creek as well as via satellite broadcast to over one hundred locations across North America, this event is designed to increase the leadership effectiveness of pastors, ministry staff, volunteer church leaders, and Christians in the marketplace.

- **Ministry-Specific Conferences**—throughout each year the WCA hosts a variety of conferences and training events—both at Willow Creek's main campus and offsite, across the U.S., and around the world—targeting church leaders and volunteers in ministry-specific areas such as: evangelism, small groups, preaching and teaching, the arts, children, students, women, volunteers, stewardship, raising up resources, etc.

- **Willow Creek Resources®**—provides churches with trusted and field-tested ministry resources in such areas as leadership, evangelism, spiritual formation, spiritual gifts, small groups, stewardship, student ministry, children's ministry, the use of the arts-drama, media, contemporary music —and more.

- **WCA Member Benefits**—includes substantial discounts to WCA training events, a 20 percent discount on all Willow Creek Resources®, *Defining Moments* monthly audio journal for leaders, quarterly *Willow* magazine, access to a Members-Only section on WillowNet, monthly communications, and more. Member Churches also receive special discounts and premier services through WCA's growing number of ministry partners—Select Service Providers—and save an average of $500 annually depending on the level of engagement.

For specific information about WCA conferences, resources, membership, and other ministry services contact:

Willow Creek Association
P.O. Box 3188
Barrington, IL 60011-3188
Phone: 847-570-9812
Fax: 847-765-5046
www.willowcreek.com

Continue building your new community!
New Community Series
BILL HYBELS AND JOHN ORTBERG
with Kevin and Sherry Harney

Exodus: *Journey Toward God* 0-310-22771-2

Parables: *Imagine Life God's Way* 0-310-22881-6

Sermon on the Mount¹: *Connect with God* 0-310-22884-0

Sermon on the Mount²: *Connect with Others* 0-310-22883-2

Acts: *Build Community* 0-310-22770-4

Romans: *Find Freedom* 0-310-22765-8

Philippians: *Run the Race* 0-310-22766-6

Colossians: *Discover the New You* 0-310-22769-0

James: *Live Wisely* 0-310-22767-4

1 Peter: *Stand Strong* 0-310-22773-9

1 John: *Love Each Other* 0-310-22768-2

Revelation: *Experience God's Power* 0-310-22882-4

Look for New Community at your local Christian bookstore.

Continue the Transformation
Pursuing Spiritual Transformation
JOHN ORTBERG, LAURIE PEDERSON,
AND JUDSON POLING

Grace: *An Invitation to a Way of Life* 0-310-22074-2

Growth: *Training vs. Trying* 0-310-22075-0

Groups: *The Life-Giving Power of Community* 0-310-22076-9

Gifts: *The Joy of Serving God* 0-310-22077-7

Giving: *Unlocking the Heart of Good Stewardship* 0-310-22078-5

Fully Devoted: *Living Each Day in Jesus' Name* 0-310-22073-4

Look for Pursuing Spiritual Transformation at your local Christian bookstore.

TOUGH QUESTIONS

Garry Poole and Judson Poling

Softcover

How Does Anyone Know God Exists?	ISBN 0-310-24502-8
What Difference Does Jesus Make?	ISBN 0-310-24503-6
How Reliable Is the Bible?	ISBN 0-310-24504-4
How Could God Allow Suffering and Evil?	ISBN 0-310-24505-2
Don't All Religions Lead to God?	ISBN 0-310-24506-0
Do Science and the Bible Conflict?	ISBN 0-310-24507-9
Why Become a Christian?	ISBN 0-310-24508-7
Leader's Guide	ISBN 0-310-24509-5

REALITY CHECK SERIES

by Mark Ashton

Winning at Life	ISBN: 0-310-24525-7
Leadership Jesus Style	ISBN: 0-310-24526-5
When Tragedy Strikes	ISBN: 0-310-24524-9
Sudden Impact	ISBN: 0-310-24522-2
Jesus' Greatest Moments	ISBN: 0-310-24528-1
Hot Issues	ISBN: 0-310-24523-0
Future Shock	ISBN: 0-310-24527-3
Clear Evidence	ISBN: 0-310-24746-2

We want to hear from you. Please send your comments about this book to us in care of zreview@zondervan.com. Thank you.

ZONDERVAN™

GRAND RAPIDS, MICHIGAN 49530 USA

WWW.ZONDERVAN.COM